Book
Lures
Inc.

FIRST RESEARCH PROJECTS
K-3
by
Nancy Polette

Illustrated by Jodi Barklage

Adapted from <u>The Research Book For Gifted Programs</u>, Book Lures, Inc., 1984 by Nancy Polette. Contributing author, Flora Wyatt.

Publisher: Book Lures, Inc.
Box 9450
O'Fallon, MO
63366

Printed by
GATEWAY PRINTING, INC.
4610 Planned Industrial Drive
St. Louis, MO 63120
(314) 261-7115

Published in U.S.A.
ISBN 0-913839-30-2

FROM A + Z

FIRST RESEARCH PROJECTS
K - 3

INTRODUCTION

Research activities for primary students are largely teacher selected. However, these activities can be done independently by the student if structured for success.

FIRST RESEARCH PROJECTS is designed to foster success experiences by providing activities that are initially based on observation and easy recording, then moving to book research projects which again call for observation and recording rather than extensive reading.

HOW TO USE THIS BOOK

Pages 1-7:   Observational research activities requiring simple resources make a good beginning. Each activity can become a part of a beginning research center set up on a classroom table.

Pages 8-14:   Duplicate the pages to make a research booklet for each child. The questions can be answered in **any** book on each topic pictured. Children can work in the booklet in **any** order. They do not have to begin with A for alligator.

Pages 15-21:   Here are beginning research projects requiring the use of either the dictionary or the encyclopedia and motivated by the initial sharing of popular picture books.

Pages 22-30:   Now we are ready for research with specific questions based on particular titles of popular non-fiction. Some questions call for "right" answers. Others require analysis and different responses on the part of the young researcher.

HAPPY RESEARCHING!

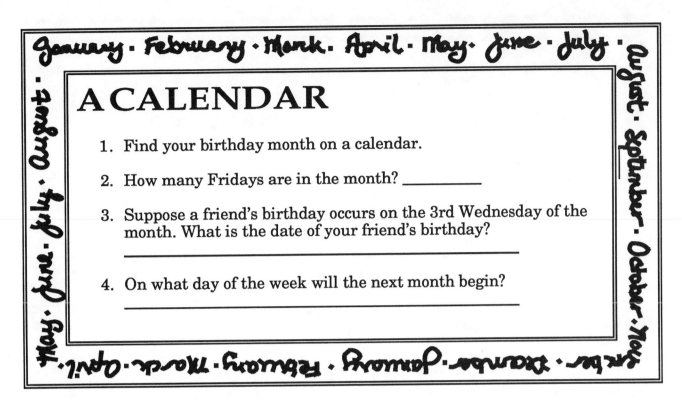

A CALENDAR

1. Find your birthday month on a calendar.

2. How many Fridays are in the month? _____

3. Suppose a friend's birthday occurs on the 3rd Wednesday of the month. What is the date of your friend's birthday?

   _____

4. On what day of the week will the next month begin?

   _____

HAIR

snake bear duck cow fish horse

1. How many girls in your class have long hair? _____
   Short hair? _____

2. Is long or short hair more popular in your class? _____

3. Circle the names of animals that have hair or fur.

snake	cow	rabbit	turtle
bear	fish	lizard	fox
duck	horse	chicken	armadillo

HOMES

1. How many homes are on the street where you live? Count the homes on one block. _____

2. Look at homes on your way to school. What color do you see most? _____

3. What building material is most used in the homes on your street? _____

4. If you could add one room to your home what room would it be? _____

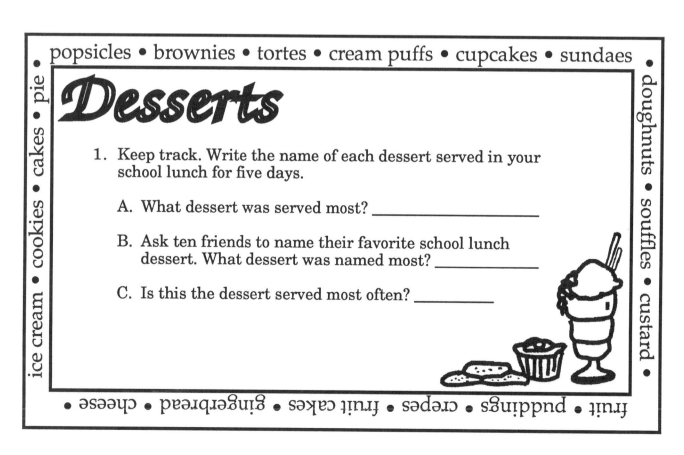

popsicles • brownies • tortes • cream puffs • cupcakes • sundaes

Desserts

1. Keep track. Write the name of each dessert served in your school lunch for five days.

   A. What dessert was served most? _____

   B. Ask ten friends to name their favorite school lunch dessert. What dessert was named most? _____

   C. Is this the dessert served most often? _____

ice cream • cookies • cakes • pie •

• doughnuts • souffles • custard •

• fruit • puddings • crepes • fruit cakes • gingerbread • cheese •

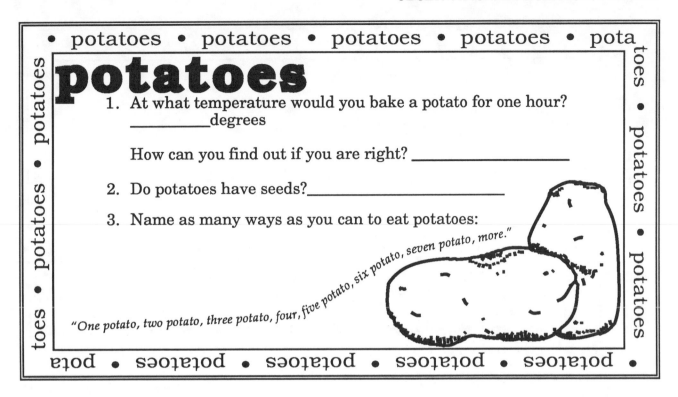

• potatoes • potatoes • potatoes • potatoes • pota

potatoes

1. At what temperature would you bake a potato for one hour?
   _____degrees

   How can you find out if you are right? _____

2. Do potatoes have seeds?_____

3. Name as many ways as you can to eat potatoes:

   "One potato, two potato, three potato, four, five potato, six potato, seven potato, more."

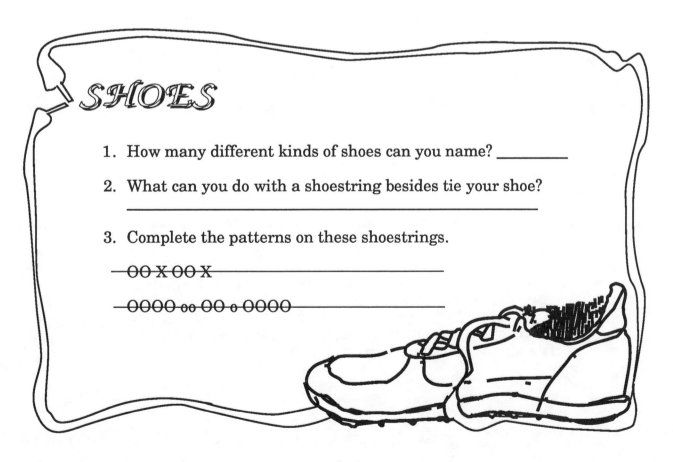

SHOES

1. How many different kinds of shoes can you name? _____

2. What can you do with a shoestring besides tie your shoe?
   _____

3. Complete the patterns on these shoestrings.

   OO X OO X _____

   OOOO oo OO o OOOO _____

A Soda Straw

1. Name three things you can drink with a straw.

   _____ _____ _____

2. Name one other thing you could do with a straw.

   _____

3. Divide 12 soda straws into two groups. How many different groups can you make? _____

4. Create something new with your twelve soda straws.

Balls

1. Name six different kinds of balls.

   _____   _____

   _____   _____

   _____   _____

2. Look at the balls used on your school playground. Which ball is used the most? _____

3. Think of a new game you could play with a ball. Tell your friends about the new game and play it with them.

apples • oranges • coconuts • grapes •

Learning About Apples

Observe three apples cut in half

1. Remove the seeds from one apple (two halves). How many seeds does it have? _____

2. Do all apples have the same number of seeds? _____

3. How can you find out?
   _____

4. Were you right? _____

5. Tell three ways an apple is like a banana.
   _____
   _____
   _____

6. Tell three ways an apple is like a stoplight?
   _____
   _____
   _____

7. List things you might see if you built a treehouse in an apple tree.
   _____
   _____
   _____

8. Divide a set of eight apples into as many different groups as you can make. How many groups did you make? _____

peaches • apricots • apples • oranges • coconuts

1. How many children are in your class? _____

2. How many children are in each of three other classes in your school? (1) _____ (2) _____ (3) _____

3. Do all classes have the same number of students? _____

4. Observe the playground at recess.

   Where do the boys play most? _____

   Where do the girls play most? _____

   Are there more boys or girls on the playground? _____

5. Name living things you see on the playground that are not children.

   _____   _____

   _____   _____

6. Name one way your playground could be made a better place to play.

   _____

7. Observe the teachers in your school. How many are men? ____ How many are women? _____ Do men teach more upper grade classes or lower grade classes? _____

8. Take a survey. Ask twenty students what time each would like school to start. Record the answers. What answer appears most often? Report your results to the school principal.

   Most students feel that school should start at _____ o'clock.

Windows and Doors

1. How many windows are in your house?

   _____

2. How many windows are in your classroom?

   _____

3. Take a survey:

   How many doors can you find in your school building? _____

   How many of these doors lead outside? _____

   Do most doors open into a room or away from a room? _____

4. How many different kinds of doors can you think of?

   _____

   _____

   _____

   _____

   _____

5. If you could open a door and enter a very special place, what place would it be?

   _____

ABCs OF NON-FICTION RESEARCH

A book of non-fiction gives factual information on a topic.

Find a Book About   **Answer These Questions**

Alligators

1. Name one enemy of the alligator.
   _____

2. Why do alligators *not* live in Alaska?
   _____
   _____

Brain

1. How many parts does your brain have?
   _____

2. What does your brain let you do that animals cannot do?
   _____
   _____

Caves

1. What rock formations hang from the ceiling of some caves?
   _____

2. What would be the most important thing for you to take into a cave?
   _____

Dinosaurs

1. What was the biggest dinosaur?
   _____

2. How do we know what dinosaurs look like?
   _____
   _____

ABCs OF NON-FICTION RESEARCH

Find a Book About	*Answer These Questions*
Eskimos	1. Where do Eskimos live? 2. Name one thing an Eskimo child your age can do that you cannot do.
Forest	1. Name two kinds of trees found in a forest. 2. What is the greatest danger to a forest?
Glaciers	1. What color are glaciers? 2. Can people walk on glaciers? Why or why not?
Horses	1. Name two kinds of horses. 2. Which is smarter, a horse or a dog?

ABCs OF NON-FICTION RESEARCH

Find a Book About	Answer These Questions
Insects	1. How many legs does an insect have? _____ 2. How many legs does a spider have? _____ 3. Is a spider an insect? _____ Why or why not? _____
Jungles	1. Name three jungle animals. _____ _____ _____ 2. Why are jungles so thick with plants and trees? _____ _____
Kangaroos	1. Where do kangaroos live? _____ 2. Why do you think a mother kangaroo has a pocket and a mother rabbit does not? _____ _____
Lighthouses	1. Why do lighthouses exist? _____ 2. What does a lighthouse keeper do? _____ _____

ABCs OF NON-FICTION RESEARCH

Find a Book About	*Answer These Questions*
Microbes	1. Where can you see microbes? _____ 2. Name one good thing microbes do. _____ _____
New York City	1. Where is New York City located? _____ 2. Name two famous places you would like to visit in New York City. _____ _____
Octopus	1. How many legs does an octopus have? _____ 2. Name two places you could go to see an octopus. _____ _____
Pigs	1. Are all pigs pink? How can you prove your answer? _____ 2. Would a pig make a good pet? _____ Why or why not? _____ _____

ABCs OF NON-FICTION RESEARCH

Find a Book About	*Answer These Questions*
Queens	1. What is a Queen?
	2. Name a fairy tale Queen.
	3. Name a Queen living today.
Robots	1. Name two things a robot can do.
	2. If you had a robot, what would you have it do?
Spiders	1. What do spiders eat?
	2. Why does a spider make a web?
Teeth	1. About when does a human baby get its first tooth?
	2. How do people lose their teeth?

ABCs OF NON-FICTION RESEARCH

Find a Book About	*Answer These Questions*
UFOs	1. What does U.F.O. mean? 2. If you saw a U.F.O., what would you do?
Volcanoes	1. Name a city that was covered by volcanic ash. 2. Could your city be covered by volcanic ash? 3. Why or why not?
Whales	1. How do we know a whale is not a fish? 2. How much can a large whale weigh? 3. What do whales eat?
Xylophones	1. What are xylophone bars made of? 2. What would you hold in your hand to play the xylophone? 3. Why do the bars on a xylophone make different sounds?

ABCs OF NON-FICTION RESEARCH

Find a Book About	*Answer These Questions*
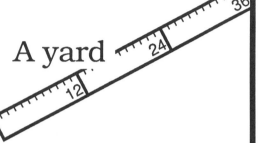 A yard	1. How long is a yard in feet? _____ In inches? _____ 2. Name things we buy by the yard. _____ _____ _____
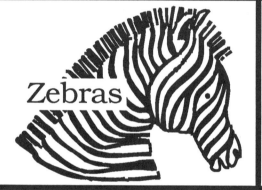 Zebras	1. In what country are zebras found running wild? _____ 2. How fast can a zebra run? _____ 3. What other animal might you see near a wild zebra? _____

Now that you have successfully completed this ABC research project, write your own ABCs of Research for someone else to solve.

"now I know my ABCs..."

ENCYCLOPEDIA RESEARCH

THERE WAS AN OLD WOMAN
by Steven Kellogg

Rosebud is enraged by a very pesty fly. While trying to kill the fly, she inadvertently swallows it. To stop the fly jiggling, she swallows a spider to catch it. Then she has to swallow a bird to catch the wriggling spider. In her desperation, she swallows many predators who in turn become prey. She meets her end by swallowing a great horse at a circus.

Prey are animals who are killed and usually devoured by predators.

Draw a line between predators and prey.

fox	fly	purple martin	lamb
spider	rabbit	lion	gazelle
owl	mouse	dingo	mosquito

Use a predator and its prey to create a poem.

There was an old man who gobbled a _____.
That leaped and creeped and leaped inside him.
He gobbled the _____ to catch the _____.
I wonder why
He gobbled a _____.
Poor old man, he's sure to die.

There was an old man who gobbled a _____.
How silly
To gobble a _____.
He gobbled the _____ to catch the _____.
That leaped and creeped and leaped inside him.
I wonder why
He gobbled a _____.
Poor old man, he's sure to die.

How can you continue this poem?

There Was An Old Woman
by Steven Kellogg, published by

Parents Magazine Press 1974

15

FORECASTING

ENCYCLOPEDIA RESEARCH

NOEL THE COWARD
published by Windmill Books
1977

NOEL THE COWARD
by Robert Kraus

Noel Kangaroo is tired of hearing the taunts of his peers. He goes to a karate school to learn to protect himself and gain courage. No longer do the others dare call Noel a coward!

Animals have unique ways of protecting themselves from predators. Some use teeth, claws, or feet. Some can outrun or outreach their predators. The armadillo wears his own impenetrable armor. Some prey rely on camouflage; rarely will a bird eat a viceroy butterfly after sampling its look-alike kin, the monarch butterfly. The walking stick insect is difficult to see upon a tree trunk.

Make up riddles about animals and the way they protect themselves. Write them below, then cut them out and staple them into a riddle book to enjoy. Add as many pages as you want!

Riddle:	Answer:
What is skinny, grey-brown, an insect, and hides on trees?	A walking stick

Riddle:	Answer:
	An opossum

Riddle:	Answer:
	A gander

Riddle:	Answer:
	A chamelon

ENCYCLOPEDIA RESEARCH

<u>FROG AND TOAD ARE FRIENDS</u>
published by Harper & Row
1970

<u>FROG AND TOAD ARE FRIENDS</u>
by Arnold Lobel

Frog and Toad have five adventures in this book. When Toad oversleeps the early spring, Frog wakes him. When Frog is ill, Toad amuses him by trying to think of a story. Together they hunt a lost button, go swimming, and await a hoped-for letter.

Frogs and toads are amphibians. They spend part of their lives on land and part in the water. Frogs have smooth, damp skin while toads have dry, bumpy skin. Toads are fatter than frogs and can't jump as far. Both lay eggs in the water – the toads in black strings and the frogs in bunches.

These words tell about frogs and toads:

gills	hibernate	croak
tail	eggs	jump
hop	lungs	bumpy
moist	dry	amphibian
string	tadpoles	cluster
climb	smooth	

1. Put a green circle around words that tell about frogs.
2. Put a brown circle around words that tell about toads.
3. Put an orange circle around words that tell about both.
4. Tell whether you would rather have a frog or a toad for
   a pet. _____
   Tell why _____

FLEXIBILITY

ENCYCLOPEDIA RESEARCH

BABAR'S CASTLE
published by Random House, Inc.
1962

BABAR'S CASTLE
by Laurent de Brunhoff

Exciting adventures happen to Babar's family when they move into Castle Bonnetrompe. The children have fights in armor and discover a secret passage.

Elephants are Earth's largest land animals. They may be eleven feet tall and weigh six tons. Because they are very intelligent and adaptable they have been used by man for thousands of years. Elephants live in large herds and are led by a wise older cow.

Learn about the African and Asiatic elephants in the encyclopedia.

These words tell about them:

large ears	two lobes on trunk
one lobe on trunk	lives in Asia
five toenails on front foot	medium ears
bowed-out back	four toenails on front foot
sloping forehead	dip behind shoulders
rough trunk	bulging forehead
lives in Africa	smooth trunk

1. Circle the words in red that tell about Asiatic elephants.

2. Box the words in green that tell about the African elephants.

ENCYCLOPEDIA RESEARCH

THE WEB IN THE GRASS
published by Scribner
1972

THE WEB IN THE GRASS
by Berniece Freschet

The dangers in the life of a spider become apparent as a small spider spins her web to await her dinner. She is hunted by many predators but she survives to lay her eggs. The story concludes her life cycle by showing her spiderlings floating to new homes.

Spiders belong to the phylum "Arthropoda." They have two body parts — the head and abdomen. Unlike insects, they have eight legs. Spiders live in many places above, on, and below the ground. Some build webs; some dig holes, and some live in water. Most spiders are not poisonous to humans.

Learn about spiders in the encyclopedia or in books with the Dewey Decimal number 595.

These words name spiders:

Trapdoor Spider

Banded Garden Spider

Orchard Spider

Black Widow Spider

Tarantula

Spring-bellied Orb Weaver Spider

Funnel-web Spider

Bird-eating Spider

Wolf Spider

Brown Recluse Spider

Crab Spider

Green Lynx Spider

Jumping Spider

European Water Spider

1. Underline those that live in bushes and plants.
2. Circle those that live below or on the ground.
3. Box in those that live in the water.
4. Draw a wavy line under those that are poisonous to man.

Which spider is the most fascinating to you?

FLEXIBILITY

ENCYCLOPEDIA RESEARCH

THE CROOKED COLT
published by MacMillan Co.
1966

THE CROOKED COLT
by C. W. Anderson

One spring on a fine horse farm a mare gave birth to a colt that was lame. He could barely stand at first. The other colts wore halters with shiny name plates, but the crooked colt wasn't even named. With courage and practice the colt overcame his handicap and became the fastest colt in the pasture.

There are around 300 breeds of horses and ponies around the world. They have held an important place in history. They have been ridden in battles, used for transportation, and trained to do work. They have been used in sports and for pets. In some parts of the world, horses are a source of food.

These words tell about horses. How many more can you add?

Palamino	foal	Appaloosa
tack	saddle	colt
trot	Morgan	canter
Lipizzaner	halter	Clydesdale
gallop	walk	filly
curry comb	stirrup	bridle
Arab	thoroughbred	mane
fetlock	muzzle	hoof

_____   _____   _____

_____   _____   _____

_____   _____   _____

_____   _____   _____

_____   _____   _____

ENCYCLOPEDIA RESEARCH   FLEXIBILITY

MR. YOWDER AND THE GIANT BULL SNAKE
by Glen Rounds

Zebulon Yowder eked out a living by painting signs on wagontrains. As he camped by
the Powder River, he noticed a newly hatched bull snake trying to crawl in his blanket
roll. Mr. Yowder befriends him by speaking in snake. Knute the Snake exercised like
Teddy Roosevelt and grew to a great size. The tale relates how Knute came to be a
buffalo hunter for the U. S. Government.

Snakes are the most widespread and numerous of the cold-blooded reptiles. Unlike
lizards, they don't have ear openings on their heads. They smell with their tongue by
poking it into special odor detectors in the roof of their mouth. Only a few snakes are
dangerous; most are beneficial to man by eating rodents.

A. Learn about snakes by searching in books with the Dewey Decimal number 598.1.
    Then decide if these superstitions or statements are true or false. Circle the correct
    letter.

    T   F   A snake's bottom jaw can separate from its top jaw.
    T   F   Some snakes hatch their eggs inside their bodies.
    T   F   A snake with its head cut off lives until sunset.
    T   F   Snakes feel movements in the ground with their body.
    T   F   A snake can catch you if you run.
    T   F   Most people die from copperhead bites.
    T   F   A milksnake can milk a cow.
    T   F   Most snakes eat their prey alive.

B. If you were a farmer, what kind of snake would you prefer in your barn?

    _____

    Why? _____

MR. YOWDER AND THE GIANT BULL SNAKE
published by Holiday House
1978

ALLIGATORS

A. Make a list of some enemies of the alligator.

B. Draw a picture of an alligator and write three interesting sentences about it.

BIGFOOT

A. Do you believe any of the stories about Bigfoot are true? Write about what you believe. Be sure to tell why you believe this way.

B. Why do you think this monster some people believe in is called Bigfoot? Write some reasons for this name being used to describe the monster.

C. Some people do not believe there is such a monster. Write some reasons about why they think there is no Bigfoot monster.

THE BOTTOM OF THE SEA

A. If you could be a diver, what would you like to look for and learn about in the sea? Write about being a diver.

B. There are things other than plants and animals which can be found in the sea or ocean. Make a list of other things in the ocean.

C. Would you like to be in a sealab or a submarine? Write about why or why not.

D. Choose one interesting animal who lives in the ocean. Write about why this animal is unusual.

THE BRAIN

A. Make list of things your brain helps you do.

B. Make a picture of the brain and a picture of a computer. Which one is the smartest? Write why you think so.

COCOA AND CHOCOLATE

A. Make a picture story showing where a chocolate bar comes from. Begin with a seed being planted in the ground.

B. If you could invent a new delicious food made from chocolate, what would it be? Make a picture of it and write an advertisement for it.

DINOSAURS

A. Making a dinosaur exhibit is almost like working a puzzle. Write about what has to be done by writing what comes first, second, and so on.

B. Draw a picture of your favorite dinosaur. Write two interesting facts about this dinosaur.

EARLY INDIANS

A. How do you know about how the earliest men in our country of America lived? Make some drawings to show what has been found to tell us about them. Label your drawings.

B. Do you think these early Americans were smart people? Write some reasons about why or why not?

C. We do not really know why the Pueblos left the cities they built in the cliffs. Even people today have to move sometimes. Write some reasons why we sometimes have to move to other places today.

ESKIMOS

A. Make a drawing of a sledge, an umiak or kayak. Write a sentence about what your drawing was used for.

B. Choose one thing the Eskimos did which you think was the most unusual. Draw a picture and write some sentences about this unusual thing.

C. Would you like to be an Eskimo? Write about why you would or would not and make a picture about your reasons.

FORESTS

A. Make a time line showing how a forest starts and changes.

B. A forest has many trees and many other living things. Make a picture of some other things which live in the forest. Write some sentences about the things you would like to see.

C. Find a list of rules about things you should not do in the forest. Make a list of things you can do in the forest.

JUNGLES

A. Why do you think plants grow so well in a jungle? Write about it.

B. Draw some animals which live in the jungle. Write their names too.

C. What is the most interesting thing to you in the jungle?   Make a picture and tell why it is the most interesting.

D. How does the jungle help us? Name one way.

KANGAROOS

A. Which animal in this book is the most interesting to you? Tell why and make a picture of it.

B. If something should happen to the mother animal soon after her baby was born, what do you think would happen to the baby? Write about it.

LIGHTHOUSES

A. Make a list about all the dangerous things which could happen to a lighthouse.

B. Which lighthouse in this book you read would you most like to have visited? Tell about your visit there.

THE LOCH NESS MONSTER

A. Do you think the Loch Ness Monster (if there is any) is a mammal, a fish, a mollusk, a reptile or an amphibian? Circle your answer. Then write why you think this way.

B. Choose an animal group. Circle your choice: mammal, reptile, amphibian, fish, mollusk. Make a picture showing what these kinds of animals are like. Write some facts about your picture.

MAMMOTHS

A. How do scientists know what the woolly mammoth looked like? Write a sentence and draw a picture about it.

B. Make a picture and write a sentence telling some things we know about mammoth hunters.

C. Make a list of ways the mammoth hunters used the woolly mammoth.

D. Do you think we may see a woolly mammoth? Why or why not?

MESSAGES

A. Choose one way messages can be sent. Write about why you think this is an interesting way to send messages.

B. Make some pictures which show how you get messages every day.

C. Make up a message you think is being sent by someone in this book. It can be a lighthouse message, smoke signal or any other.

MICROBES

A. Microbes can grow by getting so big they split in half and make two microbes. If you could split in half and grow into another person, you would have a twin exactly like yourself. Give your twin a name and tell about her or him.

B. How could you grow some microbes so you could look at them more closely? Write a plan for growing microbes.

C. Some microbes are good and some are bad. Choose good microbes or bad microbes. Write about what these microbes can do.

OCTOPUS

A. Make a list of true things about an octopus.
Hint: eight legs

B. A baby octopus hatches from an egg. Some babies are born from their mothers' bodies. Name some of each kind.

C. Write a riddle about the octopus to see if your friends can guess what sea animal you are describing.

OXYGEN

A. Make a list of places people go that they have to take oxygen with them in order to stay alive.

B. Make a drawing showing how man, fish and leaves get oxygen from the air. Label the parts you have drawn.

THE PLANETS

A. The sun and the nine planets are in space. Make a list of some other objects in space. Make a picture to show what the objects on your list look like.

B. If the planets were going to have a race to see who could go around the sun the fastest, who would win?

C. If it were possible for people to live on another planet, which one would you choose?

ROBOTS

A. Make a list of interesting things real robots can do. On the back of your paper, make a list of things you can think of that real robots cannot do.

B. Make a picture of a robot you would like to build. It can be real, like the Disneyland and Disney World robots or it can be like the robots in Star Wars. Write some things your robot can do.

C. Pretend that you could have a robot who comes to school with you. Make a list of all the things you want your robot to do for you at school.

SEAHORSES

A. How does a seahorse eat? Make a picture of a seahorse eating something – and write about how he does this.

B. Would you like to have eyes like a seahorse? Tell what you could do if you had seahorse eyes!

C. What does the male seahorse do that most other animals do not do? Write about it.

SPIDERS

A. Make a list of words that describe spiders.

B. What kind of spider do you think is the most interesting? Make a picture of it and tell why you think this spider is interesting.

C. List some ways spiders are helpful and some ways spiders are harmful to us.

D. Which kind of web is the most interesting to you? Draw a web for us to see.

THE UNIVERSE

A. Write a sentence telling why you would or would not like to live on Mars. Make a drawing of the space ship which helped us learn about Mars and write the name of this ship.

B. Choose one of the planets you are most interested in. Make a drawing of it and write some sentences which describe what this planet is like.

C. Imagine that it is a dark night and you can see a constellation (group of stars). Draw a picture of something a family of stars could show. Make the stars and draw lines between them to show your pictures.

VOLCANOES

A. Two cities which were covered by volcanic ash about 2000 years ago? Do you think your city will ever be covered with ash from a volcano? Write about why or why not.

B. If you lived near a volcano and had to leave your home, what things would you choose to take with you? Make a list.

RESEARCH CARDS

1-3

WHALES

A. Some people say there soon may be no whales left. Write about what man can do to save the whales from all dying out.

B. Make a list of facts which help us know that whales are not just fish.

C. Write some facts about the whale you found the most interesting. Make a picture to show what this whale looks like.

(YOUR TOPIC)

Write two questions about a topic you choose.

ZOO BABIES

A. Choose one animal found in a zoo that you think does something unusual. Write about what makes this animal unusual and make a picture of it.

B. Of all the zoo workers, which one would you most like to be? Tell why.

C. Do you think being in a zoo is good or bad for animals? Tell why.

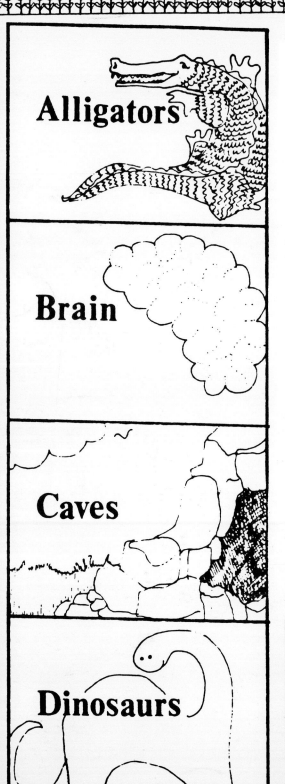

Alligators

Brain

Caves

Dinosaurs

FIRST RESEARCH

PROJECTS

K-3

contains selected activities from two other Book Lures' publications, HOW MANY BONES IN A BEAR and THE RESEARCH BOOK FOR GIFTED PROGRAMS. These beginning research activities stress hands- on, observational research as the initial research experience. Students are then moved from observing and drawing conclusions to book research with emphasis on picture books and beginning encyclopedia projects. For additional books in this series write for a free catalog to Book Lures, Inc.

Book Lures Inc.

P.O. BOX 9450
O'FALLON, MO.

63366

Horses

ISBN 0-913839-30-2